Advance Praise for
The Five Stages of Stuttering

The Five Stages of Stuttering is by far, one of the strongest voices of an emerging poet that I have read. Language lulls and sings. There is a linguistic playfulness despite the speaker's losses, both psychological and physical. The musicality and successful use of experimental forms, paired with a poignant reality, provide insight and wisdom.

—**Sheryl Luna**, author of *Magnificent Errors, Seven, Pity the Drowned Horse*

A fearless examination of grief and trauma stretching like a shadow across the speaker's language. The poems weave this shadow in patterns of silence and noise with unique syntax and repetition. They define again and again the source of grief in attempts to exorcise it. Despite the resistance of their stutter, these poems scream — are chants and spells toward healing. "I'm a singing hammer / wanting to be beautiful again —" Holguin-Pettinato writes. This is an exquisite collection!

—**Aldo Amparán**, author of *Brother Sleep*

THE FIVE STAGES

STAGES

OF STUTTERING

POEMS BY

CASSIE HOLGUIN-PETTINATO

The Five Stages of Stuttering

FLOWERSONG
PRESS

poems by

Cassie Holguin-Pettinato

FLOWERSONG
PRESS

Preface

As much time as I spend thinking about my trauma, talking about my trauma, and living with it, I haven't truly stopped to feel it. Stuttering was the sacred language that forced me to pause. I was inspired by the idea of writing poetry around this theme after watching a video segment called *Adapt-Ability*. I connected the common disfluencies in speech – repetitions, prolongations, blocks, interjections, and revisions to the stages of grief. I also did some of my own research. After a lot of trial and error, I figured out ways to write out an actual stutter and create emotional stuttering around my trauma. Initially, it was my grief that ushered me into this book, and one by one I took the poems by the hand and walked through denial, anger, bargaining, depression, and acceptance. The experience of putting myself in that space in such a short amount of time, though painful brought a deeper understanding of the grief I carry. Healing hurts and I still have moments of overwhelming grief but as uncomfortable and agonizing as that can be, it's necessary to feel it and grow around the wound. *The Five Stages of Stuttering* helped me process the pain so I could begin to write about new things and search for joy while living with a stutter.

table of contents

Stage 3: Blocks

Stage 4: Interjections

Stage 5: Revisions

"all my grief says the same thing:
this isn't how it's supposed to be.
this isn't how it's supposed to be.
and the world laughs.
holds my hope by the throat.
says:
but this is how it is"

—**Fortesa Latifi**

The Five Stages of Stuttering

Stage 1:
Repetitions

"Where—where—where did it all go wrong?"

In The Beginning,

She crawled into the darkness and followed the sounds of kittens.
When she came back to earth, she handed me the litter, and we
discovered time and space cut off the circulation and amputated
a limb, a tail, and an ear. My eyes didn't look away. I fell in
love with the three kittens whose parts were missing. I saw beauty
in a design that was not finished, the way a body can survive.
I couldn't ignore the universe calling me to care for the orphans.
The moment my father walked through the door, he was an asteroid
entering the earth's orbit, coming to end life. He violently put them
in a box and left them next door, creating a crater inside of me.
You could argue it wouldn't have been good to keep sick kittens.
You could argue I would have gotten sick. You could argue he was
protecting me. I was seven years old. I knew what kind of man he
was before this day: one who would not take the time to talk to me,
take the kittens to the vet, and find a home. One who would not care
for orphans, a border crosser, a crying child, a sick animal. Before
the foundation of the earth, his heart was made of hard clay, silicate
rocks, and metals. I didn't have the voice to break apart the asteroid
and save the kittens.

Leo Season

It was your desperate plea, your adolescent voice,
the phone cord wrapped around my neck
that made me say yes to meeting you at the portables
at school.

The Misfits lyrics in the background underscored
your message, *Die, die, die, my darling,*
as you got out of the car and changed your work
shirt to a death metal t-shirt.

I blushed at the sight of your arms and bony shoulders,
the outline of your lungs and hips, and your calloused
fingertips running through your hair.
I looked straight into you and went blind.

You came towards me like a crashing planet and spoke
in rhythms – I was your girlfriend. You held my hand
as we crossed the street, but I didn't want to hold yours.
I didn't know you. I didn't know myself.

I didn't know my freshman year would be a purple bruise.
I would be filled with stomach pains and searching
for you like a lost sun. Those days would split me open.
I didn't know I would never see again.

Confirmed Diagnosis

My OB-GYN does a cotton swab test because the burning.
Stinging.Stabbing.Itching.Rawness.Throbbing.Won't.Stop.
She gently pokes over parts of my vulva, and I tell her where
I feel the most pain. It was agonizing. Too excruciating to
ignore. <u>Diagnosis</u>: Vulvodynia (vul-vo-DIN-ee-a) – Un-
explained chronic vulva pain and pain at the opening of the vagina.
<u>Possible causes</u>: Injury to the nerves, long-term reactions to past
vaginal infections, weakened pelvic floor muscles, spasms. Sexual
abuse, sex without enough lubrication and readiness, childbirth, riding
in the car with a man with road rage, impatience, and a lack of empathy.
<u>Treatments</u>: creams and ointments to numb the vulva, and stabilize
the nerves, antidepressants, anti-convulsants, nerve blocks – injections
that prevent pain signals from traveling from the nerves to your
brain, physical therapy – loosens muscle tension in your pelvic floor.
Counseling for emotional pain. Or attempt to deal with it, but
you can't. <u>Heal time</u>: Never.

Corp's Hymn

From the Halls of Montezuma
I can't tell the similarities between
a leather belt / his words / venom &
To the shores of Tripoli, honey /
villain & / brother / *We fight*
our country's battles / a snake with a twin /
a Cancer / *In the air, on land,*
and sea; / a Gemini / jarhead / man
who defiles / *First to fight for right and*
freedom / little sister / enemy / friend /
who keeps secrets / *And to keep*
our honor clean; / a dirty wound / an honor /
shoot / cease-fire / cease-fire / traitor / sister /
stranger / *We are proud to claim* / a lie /
the truth / *the title Of United States Marine.*

The First Year of Pentimento

*Pentimento— a visible trace of an earlier painting beneath
layers of paint on a canvas.*

I let her marry us | The wife of the man | who tried to rape me | She doesn't know
what happened | I knew | from the start | This cursed us | I knew | I knew | I knew.

Sex was painful | on our wedding night | Maybe because we weren't in | our home |
I didn't want to spend the night | at the missionary's house | My anxious feet | ran | We
had to move the next day | You worked the next day | leaving me alone with boxes.

The missionary fights me | She shames me | with an old Bible | passage | The two shall |
become one flesh | Leave | and cleave | Leave and cleave | Leave and cleave.

I'm alone in the apartment | still | full of boxes | I lost myself | I think about | the litter
of kittens | I found | missing body parts. | Not knowing | I'm going to become | your
new mother | I'm going to be | the one | who keeps us alive.

You leap | from our bed | go to a job | you hate | You ring | hollow and discarded | I
watch | from the window | children picking flowers | I don't want to | accept this pain |
on the morning altar | We never had | a honeymoon | I haven't seen | you | smile for days.

The honesty | my sunflower | bouquet dying | hurts my eyes | Twice I've felt rejected | I
want to cleave to | you | my husband | a delicate flame | I'm left alone to | search for more
wood | Leave and cleave | Leave and cleave | Leave and cleave.

You're accused | crimes of the past | questioned | humiliated | guilty until | proven
innocent | Isn't allowed | at church | Ex-girlfriend will kill herself | if she sees you | I still
go | I have to | be silent

My wedding | shoes have holes | as big as | the nails that went | through Jesus' feet | Each
morning the dishes pile up | I pretend not to | see them | I look | at the 3rd ring
you gave me | The first one fell | out of your pocket | got lost in the cemetery.

I saw you sitting | at the edge of the bedpost | I went inside the closet | I turned into |
a prayer room | I wrestle not against | flesh and blood | Forgive | they do not know | Love |
is patient | Love is kind.

You sing the blues | I play the same | three notes over | and over | We invite | the
congregation to | come to our home | worship | like in the upper room | at Pentecost | No
one showed up | no one ever shows up.

I want to be a missionary | I try to convince you | Preach | the good news | to unreached
people | the deaf | Ireland | It's just an escape | for us to leave | Cleave and leave | Cleave
and leave | Cleave and leave.

After the Depo shot | the bleeding didn't stop | I swelled | like a pale balloon | I bled | on
the altar you held me | I kneeled | they laid hands | on my body | begged for healing | and
begged for mercy.

When you lost your job | she fought you | said she would | pay for the divorce | I
convinced myself over | and over I still want to | be married I do | I do | I do | I do | We
can't pay the rent | For this reason | a woman shall | return to | her mother's house.

Confession

For you created her inmost being. You have written her name on the palm of your hands. You knit her together in my womb. Children are an inheritance from you. I praise you because she is fearfully & wonderfully made. I present my body as a living sacrifice, holy & acceptable. Your works are wonderful, I know that full well. You chose me to be her mother. Her frame was not hidden from you. I have no fear, for you are with me. When she was made in the secret place. I have hope in together in the depths of you. Your eyes saw her continue to offer a days ordained for her before one of them came nothing. How precious me, God! How vast is the anxious about anything. they would outnumber I awake, I am still with

you. When she was woven the earth. I have trust in unformed body; I will sacrifice of praise. All the were written in your book to be. In you, I lack are your thoughts about sum of them! I will not be If I were to count them, the grains of sand—when you. You know the number

> I placed the test on top of the sink, sat on the tub's edge and waited. I saw my inheritance and passport to Ireland slipping through my fingers. Rolling hills turned into sharp valleys. I wasn't happy the moment I found out I was pregnant. I didn't want to carry this child.

of hairs on her head. Every good & perfect gift is from above. I will be saved through faith. I can do all things because you give me strength. I will not labor in vain nor bear children doomed to misfortune. Your plans are to prosper me & not harm me. I will put my whole trust in you because you are for me & not against me. For you created her inmost being, I carry this joy.

Good Friday

I ripped out
all the pages from my journals.
Each page sounded like a band-aid
coming off, and my daughter
looked at me with worried eyes
as I did this. *Ouch, ouch, ouch*
she said. Ouch, to unanswered prayers,
prophecies still waiting for birth
days, visions & dreams misinterpreted,
poems & writings from the inspiration of
God. I tore it all out, the treasures I swore
I could take with me through fire.

12 years of devotion   gone

I had done this once before
after I said the sinner's prayer, I threw
all my secular treasures in trash bags
& replaced my walls with Bible passages
& the promises of

God. I'm converting back to myself and what
am I to do? What am I to do? What-what-what
am I to do but go back to where I started

I have to start where–where–
where I left off

<<< Rewind

I hear the dogs
But I don't see them
They alarm me in the night
I know it's you coming
Through my window

Stage 2:
Prolongations

"Wh-wh-wh-why does it have to be this way?"

Silent Miscarriages

I was taking
out the crust from his belly button
like I used to when we were teenagers.
I used to stick my finger deep inside
the center and fi–fi–fi–find lent and
dead skin rolled into a ball. It gave me
pleasure digging for tho-tho–tho–those
short moments cleansing his filth.
Moments, I pulled out the weirdest sh-sh-
sh–shit trapped in him. I would go too
far in a–a–a–and get carried away by the
si–si–si–silent miscarriages. Him and I
silent miscarriages.

Rogue

According to the dictionary, you're either a dishonest person or an elephant
driven away, living apart from the herd, or having destructive tendencies.

I think you were driven away from your herd, and I'm setting you off
by trying to get you to come back. My talking head about things I don't understand
creates a chemical reaction in you, and it's Uncle Sam's fault.

He took you away from me, and for what reason would you go
through such destruction, humiliation, constipation, stripped of who you are
to become a machine, ready for combat?

Your clothes are taken away, and your head is shaved; you're issued the same clothes,
respond to barking commands, eat when you're told to eat, and sleep when you're told
to sleep. If someone fucks up a duty, everyone pays for it by running around
the squad bay, looking for things amiss. You find yourself in the pit as punishment.

Everywhere you go, you are screamed at. You are screamed at to fill your canteen
faster, eat faster, pee faster, wash up faster, get back in line fast, wake up faster.

Lights! Lights! Lights!
There's no time for stretches or yawns. You get in line and are a number counted.
They beat out of you the name I loved, and at oh four hundred, you are pronounced
a metamorphosed rock, a biological catalyst ready to explode. This is what you chose,
spending most of your free time at attention, waiting for forgiveness.

Or maybe you are a destructive person because there was honesty up the hill when you
would blend into the bushes with your air rifle, pretending to be a scout sniper, waiting
to shoot birds and cats. I would hear the moment you pulled the trigger and punctured
the skin of animals without a single breath from long range. The satisfaction on your
face gushed out like a bleeding star.

Soy Chicana

Soy chicana porque mi [me] padre odia [OH - dee - yah] a los
mexicanos en este pais.

Soy chicana porque mi [me] segundo idioma [ee - deyO - mah]
es pocho, español roto sin [seen] remedio [reh - MEH - dio].

Soy chicana porque nunca he [eh] ido [E - doe] al otro lado
de la frontera, me [meh] dijieron que me [meh] tragarian [trah - gah -rEE - un].

Soy chicana porque mi [me] cuerpo siente lo que mi [me]
padre suprimio [su - prim - YO].

Soy chicana porque mi [me] dolor requiere [reh - kye - reh]
justicia [whoes-tea-cia].

Soy chicana porque mi [me] padre me [meh] llama traidora [try - door-ah].

Soy chicana porque soy hija de dos mundos pero solo me [meh]
han [an] mostrado uno.

Soy chicana porque tengo una espina dentro [den - tro] de mi [me] que quiere salir.

The Lamb's Tail Hides A Multitude Of Sins

My skin — graffiti all over a holy temple.
I never wanted to look this way — I'm a singing hammer
wanting to be beautiful again —

but I fucked up by running
away from the pain and into a tattoo shop.
Trying to cover up the unhealed spider bites.
I smashed the outer layer of my skin.
All this ink flesh to
remember. It all started because You left me.

– You escaped,
and I faced my destiny.

***

   Aching. Burning. Screaming.
   <u>New symptoms:</u>
   Pain in the joints that sit
   where the lower spine and pelvis meet,
   pinching my hip and inner thigh,
   all the way to my butt and inside.
   The sciatic nerve, the pudendal nerve
   burns and stings.
   This pain wraps around my leg,
   down to my foot till it goes numb.

***

The MRI is three days away. Deliver me
from all the evil I've done to myself.
Let the tail fall off.

The Son of Joseph and Ashikai

Ghana West Africa home to the Seventh Son
of Joseph & Ashikai Loveson was spotted by
a white missionary woman. The moment she
saw him she claimed him as her son just like that.

Before this moment when he was inside his mama's
belly, the sack ruptured, and the liquid amputated
his toes and fingers. His left hand became the shape
of love in sign language. His Mother died shortly after
and his father went missing.

The stranger came like a rat in the night and took him
out from The Sisters of Charity in Accra. Just like that,
she was his new mother. Like a flower plucked from the
earth dying in her pocket.

She took him around the world just like that
until America was home. Peter Tetteh Loveson became
Eric Nahum York. Date of birth: unknown. Age: unknown.

He lost his native tongue. Ga and Twi turned southern.
He traveled by force from church to church. This woman
paraded him around like an animal to gain support as a
missionary midwife. He was told no one wanted him, yet
he was carried on his grandmother's back. He would live
a beggar or die.

*

He called me at 2 am weeping, repeating himself over and over.

I want / my mom / she is not here / there's nothing / I can do about it

I want my mom / she is not / here / there's nothing I can do about it

I want my mom she is not / here there's nothing / I can do / about it

DeafMissions

*

Awake before she signals hunger because her cries make you sad.
Memorize her cues; when her hands start moving toward her mouth,
sacrificially give your breasts. This is all you can offer to make
up for not being there the moment she was taken into the ambulance.

*

She had to live her first week of life
in the NICU. You didn't see her for
more than an hour. You chose not to
spend the night with her at the hospital
out of fear. You weren't able to look at her
with tubes and wires. You weren't the one
who bathed her first. You weren't there
at night when she cried.

*

After she was taken, you stayed behind. The midwife closed the tear
with stitches. The burning pieces of your vagina held more weight
than wondering if she was okay or thinking about your husband in the
ambulance with blood on his clothes, hearing the driver scream
at the cars to move, and the medics in the back intubate her. He heard
as they attached the aspirator and suction catheter to the end of a tube.
They worked on her until the stained fluid was out of her lungs.

*

She is home now, and this reality
paralyzes you, and fear and anxiety
are a placenta stuck inside your
stomach. You want to run away,
take the rent money, go to Ireland
as planned, become a deafmission,
but she is home, and you don't want
motherhood.

*

You try to remember God's prophecies spoken over you, but a
traumatized mother doesn't fulfill the Word. A newborn doesn't care.
She wants to live, and you want to die. A blue demon speaks to you in
Bible riddles, taunts you in sign language, and you understand every
judgment formed against you.

*

The Little Foxes

From Song of Songs

When I loved God I could
never catch the little foxes.
Those pinche traviesos spoiled
our vineyard and trampled on
the tender grapes. They destroyed

everything that grew in the garden.

They turned the wine into dead water,
broke the anointing jar filled with Cassia,
chewed the kitchen table, and left splinters.

They pissed on the bathroom floor,
tore the silk sheets of our bed,
and the beams of our home collapsed.

They— killed God.

I still can't catch the troubling foxes,
those sly cabrones that hinder love,
that hide in the clefts of the rock.
They raid the budding vineyards
and escape with full bellies.

Stage 3:
Blocks

"I want [   ] peace."

The Way Out

I walk through the Newborn Intensive Care Unit,
a maze, a haunted house. I'm in a hurry to get the crying babies
hooked to a ███████ No one is here to care for them
　　　They ██████ when I come near
I pass by another baby with a nursing mother　　　　　I keep going further
until I reach the back of the ███████　　　　There's a deformed baby
　　　The bottom part of her body was █████　　　　her face was ████
　　　　　She was left abandoned away from ███████
Down the hall I find a nurse in a room dancing over another baby
I ask her where is the way out?
　　　　　She said, "It's not through the way you think. It only leads you to more rooms.
　　　　　　　　　The way out is ███████████

29

First Love

I ran into a church building to hide from him
because I thought barricading the door
with the blood of Jesus, the wood, and the nails
that crucified Him would save me.

Since high school, his ghosting kept me
searching for him. I told myself
—You're going and coming back
because you love me.

Everybody knew the truth, and I didn't
want to believe it.

+

In the Christian world, they call this a "stronghold"
I need the laying of hands to cast it out of me.

I hid in the Bible + when I prayed + in church +
when I repented + when I joined ministries +
when I confessed + when I prayed + repeat

I hid in the Bible + when I prayed + in church +
when I repented + when I joined ministries +
when I confessed + when I prayed + repeat

+

I could have gone to Ireland to be a missionary
And still, this crushing would have followed me there.

Nothing could have saved me from him, not even God.

The last time
After Lost Mind

1.

The last time I saw
my brother was at the airport
leaving for boot camp

      4 months   17 days

3 meals   3 countries

    2 boots   1 light, no light

                                Several written letters

7 or 8 deliveries

                  2 hands

    1 rifle

                3 or 4 photographs

1 cotton bed

                  2 seasons

                       1 god, no god

2.

The last time I saw
my brother
his head
was attached
to his body

How are you? [Tsenqah yaast]

Stop! [Woodray-jay]

Hands up! [Laasoonah portah-kay]

Get back! [Pooh shah shay]

Go! [Zay/Za]

Don't cross this line! [De khat nah meh tayra jay]

Don't talk! [Khaberray meh kaway]

Come with me! [Maasarah raazay]

Open it! [Classah kay]

Close it! [Band-kay]

I need to search you! [Mooshe gwaro cheh tasso taalaashee ko]

...or I'll shoot! [Yah zay daaz kah-way]

3.

I remember

        when we were

               able to go   out and play

I keep looking   back

            and waiting to see

     you

      I remember   the moment   you went missing

Leaving me

     with a shell

         of who you once used to be

I Don't Understand The Pain

he carries | heaviness in his breath | hip pain
walking alongside me | pain | I don't notice | pain
missing fingers and toes | I don't piece together
his body is surviving | his story | I'm angry | I'm angry
His constant wondering | orphan | beggar | orphan
husband | leads us to scramble for money | I don't
understand the lost look in his eyes | When he looks
into the mirror | there's no mama to care | care for
his coils | his searching | wh— | wh— | wh—
| wh— | wh—why | he gets easily startled | wh—why |
he wakes up | wh–why disoriented | wh—why | he sits in
silence | Wh–why my husband stares into nothing.

Becoming Salt

The memory of Jesus leaves me empty I used to be

a huntress for him I turned this room into

a sanctuary I stripped anything that wasn't of god

In this room I went into the deep it's true I used to be

a treasure in the nook of his hand until I let go so I became

the rock Moses struck twice & gushed out waters of rage &

I became John the Baptist's head on a tray & I became

the minute the rooster crowed three times &

I became the whip that drove out thieves & I became salt

Remnants: The First and The Last

I'm getting ready for tubal ligation and
when the doctor gently pulled out the IUD
I felt the pressure of the T-shaped device
travel down my uterus. When it came out,
my vagina lit up like a firefly, signaling
there were other things inside me that _____.

I did want another baby, But I had to burn
my fallopian tubes and cut off that part
of me forever. Everything I do as a mother is
for the first and last time. My body is inflamed,
tense and tight. The pain dial mode is turned
high. My brain hears everything

my mouth says. I'm more grief than woman.

Creator of Black Holes

They say that when you're in a car accident, it's worse if you see it coming. That your body preparing to shield itself creates internal harm.

*

riding in the car with my father i braced myself for death going 100mph on the freeway i braced myself for the colliding of metal a black hole and galaxies splitting open all over the pavement as he zoomed through each car and cursed i clenched my vagina and my shoulders caved in i locked my hips and sank into my pelvic cavity keeping safe the space below where the bladder rectum uterus fallopian tubes and ovaries live i tightened my whole body held on to the car door and shut my eyes my whole body went into its shell and waited for the explosion i held my breath between the in breath and out breath ive never taken a full breath even though we never crashed i haven't loosened my pelvic floor muscles i havent gone deep inside myself to pull me out i havent unclinched the fear of my fathers language and tone that leaked all over me his impatience and eye rolls the faces that made my entire body crash

Prophecies

G - - -d told me before [   ] she was born,
        she was his secret

agent. She would come into this [   ] world
        with stealth and great victory.

Instead, she blew her cover [   ]
        And nearly died. he said

she was a ram's horn [   ]
        Calling-out-the-called-out-ones-to-gather.

Instead, I isolated her [   ] he called her
        The Flash, a bolt of lightning that moves

in and out through walls. instead, she faced
        [   ] Mama's walls. G - - -d said I would

have joy the day she was born.
        Instead, I wrapped my hands around my head

and [   ] wept.

Stage 4:
Interjections

"I don't know um, how to let go."

At The Well

▶ **Play**

When I shifted my body towards his,
he asked me if I wanted to be held.

I nodded

yes. And I sighed deeply into his arms,
holding my hand over his belly,
coming here again to draw water.

∙ **Pause**

I asked him today if he could
imagine me forever. I trembled
when I asked him to stop running.
Could we start over? I promise
we will never thirst again.

∙ **Skip Foward**

The last day I saw him we watched
Prometheus and he made me laugh
at every scene. We were teenagers
again. Held down by humor.
Again, he's gone. He never says
goodbye.

▶ **Play**

As I walked through the door, my
husband saw the look on my face
And knew his answer.

• **Pause**

I cried dead springs of water.

The Shop

My father kept all the tools he ever needed to build
in his shop. Everything had its place. I loved to
sit and look at how organized this space was.
Every nail and screw in mason jars, power tools,
drills up on the wall and pieces of wood stored away
for future projects. Pictures of my brother and I
on his vision board. Tom Petty playing in the background.

*

I used to wear the body parts of my Barbie dolls as
pendants, and he saw the one I wore every day needed
fixing. He took me into the shop with a new Barbie
and prepped her for surgery. I watched him as he laid
her on the sawing board and amputated her arm.
He wiped away the debris and made a clean cut on the wrist,
then gently drilled a small hole so the beaded neckless
could go through. He put the new pendant on me, and
we both smiled at each other.

*

He was someone different in the shop. I could go
there and watch him for hours become a creator
of new galaxies. I wanted him to stay this way
But when he returned to earth, he transformed into

45

a man filled with hate. If I had spoken, I wouldn't have grown up with a father. If I had said I didn't want cereal in the morning, he would have given me a stone.

MRI

I thought of him
as I was inside
the war machine.
I closed my eyes, and I left my body.
I thought that he probably had to
do the same thing to survive.
It reminded me of a POW torturing device.
The repeating sounds of gunfire,
metal hitting metal, the sounds of crying soldiers
looking at pictures of their sons
every night. I had to dissociate —The only way
to withstand being buried alive.

I'm sorry,

I didn't realize you had to hold still, too — make up
a song in your head. While in basic training,
you jumped in 30 feet of water from 15ft high,
But you weren't there the moment mom stopped
making potato tacos with Mexican rice or vegetable soup.
You missed my college graduation,
and you've never been to any of my poetry readings.
You weren't there when Blockbuster closed
or the moment I turned into salt looking for god.

But I wasn't there — in the foxhole with you,
I wasn't there when your truck ran over an IED.
I wasn't there the moment your head hit the ground.

I wasn't there to see your finger on the trigger.
I wasn't there when the enemy approached you.
I wasn't there the moment your heart became calloused.
I wasn't there the day Johnny died.

I wasn't there for you either.

Shadows

I was delivered
the news   6 more months of winter   pain

2nd MRI
      w/contrast
          Impressions:

               A fluid-filled
               sac   like a
               cocoon
               ready   to
               hatch inside
               of me

Findings: arachnoid cyst on my spinal
cord.

                  I was born with
             a tale

             a burning vulva
               another diagnosis

s
a
y
k
r
o
e
i
l
e
i
t
i
s

Sacroiliitis: inflammation of the SI joints.

                  Again
                      I
I'm going to Ireland   will
            with   not
         pure   find
        intentions   relief
                    again

With a
broken body
with this
pain
wrapped
around my
dream

                                    I carry
                                    grief
                                    I
                                    will
                                    never
                                    be
                                    without
                                    pain

                    I'm going to Ireland

                                    with
                                this pain in
                                the hips

        with
    out the
    gospel   I'm waiting for the shadows
        with
    out Jesus   to move
        with
    a thorn   reveal its
                                          face

            I
            c   Ireland is
            a
            n   slipping through my sweaty hands again
            b
            a   this dream is a dandelion
            r
            e   through my fingers like
            l
            y   shadows
            m
            o   like a miscarriage like silk sheets
            v
            e   like ghosts who won't lay to rest
            m
            y   like holy water like a mirage like
            b
            o   quicksand through my fingers
            d
            y   like not resting in the shadow of the

                    El-Shaddai

Voice

From Psalm 29

I planned to give birth in the middle of the living room,
in a pool of water. A tabernacle to hold me. This is where
I started, not where I ended.

It began with an unexpected melody ["The voice of the LORD
makes the deer give birth and strips the forest
bare;] a growl brought ease to the shockwaves of cramps
[And in His temple, everyone says, "Glory!"] suddenly

                                                                          stops.

My midwife's voice tells me not to do that Sound.
She tells me to breathe through the pain some other way.
I become a lost rhythm. a frozen fawn. a frightened cat.
I feel the urge to let down my net and fish for my baby,
but she says not to push. ["The voice of the LORD is over

the waters"] I have to get out of the pool, and by the time
I want to go back in, the water is cold. The water is done.
The water can't hold us anymore. ["The voice of the LORD breaks
the cedars;"]

With A Needle And Thread

I stitched your wounds.
I pulled the needle through your black skin
from outside to inside,
And it was finished.

I held on when I needed to let go
of the silk braided ties holding you together.
When we divorced, I didn't want to cut the knots
And pull out the strands.

I didn't want to break —
I didn't want you to break free from me
to another home.

***

When it always came time to pack,
I placed our lives neatly inside
cardboard boxes.
I want to go through the underbrush
and pack one last time.

One last time.

A Case of Nostalgia

A. *In the 17th century, nostalgia was considered a disease by Swiss physician Dr. Johannes Hofer. As soon as it became a medical term to describe the sadness Swiss soldiers felt during the wars because they wanted to return home, they were discharged from their duties. For some, the cure was to return home; for others, there was no home to return to.*

B. *The Greek word for "return" is nostos. Algos means "suffering." So nostalgia is the suffering caused by an unpleasant yearning to return. - Milan Kundera*

I bury the living
in my mind | with no home | The ofrenda of
my heart grieves in 4
x 8, and 8 x
10 shadow boxes | I place them | on my
body. Tattoos
honoring that I once knew them |
There is no grave
to visit the living | Here | is where they
sleep,
where my dreams of them
stay in limbo.

At The Tone Leave A Message

B-e-e-e-e-p

Clearing throat

mhem

mmhm
mmhm

hem   *heum*
             heum
             him

hmm

eh-ehm

sigh

Umm..hey mama it's me.
I…I can't stop crying. I think
there's something wrong with me.
Like really wrong and everyone tells me it's
normal. This doesn't feel normal. I need help…
umm I get these thoughts that I don't want to say
out loud, but they are there, and…*deep breathe* I left her

54

crying in her crib, I just stood there and watched.
I didn't pick her up or comfort her. I wanted her to feel
umm…the agony I felt. What the fuck is wrong with me?
I don't think I should be alone with the baby.
I'm a horrible mother. I dont know how to get out
of whatever this is. Each day gets worse and worse.
god, I just want umm… help.
Umm, ok, call me back when you get a chance
…Bye

Stage 5:
Revisions

"My sadness is rotting…
It's rotting in a broken…my sadness is not the end"

A Case of Phantom Limb Pain

Phantom limb syndrome is the feeling of sensations in a limb that has been removed. The limb may feel as though it is still attached to the body. This is because the brain continues to get messages from nerves that used to "feel" for the missing limb.

He can't live / here / because the brother I grew up with is gone / he would see / his ghost too. He would see / the smoke stacks whose long gone / limbs / I remember / as if they were my own / I feel / the pain of where it belongs / I feel / it walking / in the front yard / the wheels of our bikes / turn / and / turn / and //

turn forever

Funeral Market

Chronic pain is a swollen chiffon
blouse that burns like cuts on
a bucher's hands

from slaughtering sheep
all day at the market

And I'm there to buy cloth
and bandages to help manage
the pain of the sheep that survived.

The Fourth Trimester

Birth Plan: She expected her baby to come out of the water fast with a strong cry, and at that moment, she would understand the song she carried. She would embrace her skin-to-skin, and nurse her right away. Nothing would separate them.

Newborn assessment: Heart rate: Above 100 / Breathing effort: good, crying / Muscle tone: active movements / Reflex or irritability: good cry / Color: pink

Mother's assessment: Joy

* * *

Reality: The baby's head crowns for several minutes, and shortly after, the rest of the baby is delivered. There is evidence of meconium staining on the infant's face. The midwife wraps her with a towel and places her on the mother's chest. The mother is unaware that her baby isn't breathing.

Newborn Assessment: The baby came into the world blue. She swallowed the early stool. Sticky and thick meconium aspirated into her lungs. The midwife saw death, fetal distress, a limp body, no cry, no breath, no pictures, no skin-to-skin, or nursing. Resuscitated at birth.

Mother's assessment: The mother is exhausted and dehydrated. She no longer had the strength and confidence to birth her baby the way she planned. She felt broken, defeated, and guilty, The mother can't forgive herself. She did everything she could, but she wasn't ready for the unexpected.

Operation Wetback

To preserve his life,
my father hid the sacred clown
inside him. The nuns would slap
the code talkers with a ruler,
and in those moments, he decided
to be anything but brown.

The gap between him and I grows
wider. We can't let go
of the past but for different reasons.
My body holds this against him:
The anniversary of
every time I laughed, he rolled
his eyes. My entire being filled him
with annoyance. I couldn't speak
the language of my mother, and so
I hid the sacred clown in me and became
the kittens with missing body parts.

I never wanted to hurt my father's
feelings. My truth would pierce
through the heart of the sad clown.
I had to nod yes to protect myself from
the comic explosions. I memorized his faces
and understood what an orphan needs to know.
How could I hold this against him?

I searched the earth looking for his mother
and found her. I held the hand of the one
who gave him up on the border.

I tried to save his life. I tried to
show him who is he but he is the same,
yesterday, today, and forever. Amen.

Like petrified wood, he preserves his life.
He holds on to the past to deny he was
there. I wasn't there either to see clearly.
I put up walls, I rejected him but now I can hear
his agony, his prayers for me to reach out and call.

Tá Brón Orm For A While

In Irish when you talk about emotion, you don't say, "I am sad." You'd say, "Sadness is on me"
—"Tá Brón Orm."

Sadness is on me
Maybe for a little while
Maybe for a long time, like oil
that spilled over a riverbed.

[Insert Title]

~~& I know I was the keeper of the flame,~~
~~a prophetic voice, a prayer warrior. I was a~~
~~Church girl & I miss being there filled with~~
~~The Spirit. I remember my worship to god, I danced~~
~~with silk flags. The fabric wrapped around my entire~~
~~body and I hid in the anointing oils of frankincense~~
~~and myrrh. I want to find him again.~~
I won't find Him here.

Liturgy Forever

I will always grieve
for the life
we never got to live

Weeping Willow

And I knew what you were missing
the moment I saw you, an orphan
in my presence,

I dug into you to plant a tree,
and what you gave me was a weeping
willow. Trees that are nothing more
than a twig, shortlived, trees that are
always thirsty like a teenager.

And I get it now, why you would call me,
sweetness in a can. I was your purest drug,
my body was molasses inside your belly.
I soothed your pain while you gave me
a place to feed mine. You and I were always
a brittle bark prone to break.

I will forever love you. I can't help wanting to
because, in the beginning, she crawled into
the darkness and followed the sounds of kittens....

Notes

The Five Stages of Stuttering was inspired by a film segment called Adapt-Ability (Episode 2) directed by James Robinson.

A helpful guide to writing the different stutters is from *Stuttering: A Teacher's Guide pdf* from marshall.edu.

The line in **Leo Season** *The Misfits lyrics in the background underscored your message* is taken from Donna Synder's poem, "Your Words A String Of Drunken Pearls." In the same poem, "Die, die, die, my darling" is a song by The Misfits.

Confirmed Diagnosis is composed of partial information taken from different medical sites.

Corps Hymn is taken from The United States Marine song "The Marines' Hymn."

The following lines from **Pentimento** *I wrestle not against | flesh and blood | Forgive | they do not know | Love is patient | Love is kind* is from Genesis 2:24 KJV; Ephesisnas 6:12; Luke 23:34 and 1 Corinthians 13:4–8a. In the same poem, the depo shot is a contraceptive injection that contains the hormone progestin.

Confession is taken from the following Bible passages: Psalm 139, Isaish 49:16, Psalm 127:3, Romans 12:2, Psal, 23, Philippians 4:6-13, Luke 12:7, James 1:17, Ephesians 2:8, Isaiah 65:23, Jeremiah 29:11, Romans 8:31.

The Lamb's Tail Hides A Multitude of Sins is a line referenced in my chapbook, The Lamb's Tail (Bottlecap Press, 2022). In the same poem, *Deliver me from all the evil I've done to myself* are lyrics from the song "Arms I Know So Well" by Emma Ruth Rundle.

The Son of Joseph and Ashikai is written for Peter Tetteh Loveson.

The title of **DeafMissions** is an organization that creates video content in sign language that communicates the gospel to 70 million deaf people worldwide.

The Way Out is written after Leila Chatti's poem "Etiology."

The Last Time is inspired by an interpretive dance "Lost Mind" by Sara Silkin. In the same poem part 2 was taken from The Tactical Pashto Course which is one of the three Tactical Language & Culture Training Systems used by the U.S. Military.

At the Well is a reference to John 4:18.

MRI has the same title as Leila Chatti's poem.

The information in **Nostalgia** is taken from *The Atlantic*'s article, "When Nostalgia Was A Disease."

The definition in **Phantom Limb Pain** is taken from the Western New York Urology Associates.

The Fourth Trimester is used to describe the postpartum period, defined as the first 12 weeks after delivery. It is inspired by Assessments for Newborn Babies.

Operation Wetback references the mass deportation of Mexican undocumented workers in 1954.

Tá Brón Orm taken from Poetry Unbound, a podcast hosted by Pádraig Ó Tuama in which he speaks about Danez Smith's poem "I'm going back to Minnesota where sadness makes sense."

Acknowledgments

Edward Vidaurre, Avery Castillo, Priscilla Celina Suarez, and everyone at Flowersong Press for making this possible.

Donna Synder (1955-2022) I remember everything you told me.

My poetry mentors Ysella Fulton-Slavin and Richard Yañez.

To my friends and colleagues who have shown me much support. Erika Tilley aka Poet Khan thank you for your friendship and sisterhood, Aldo Amparán, Sheryl Luna, Yvette Perez, Aliah Candia, Liz Liano, Roberto Salas, Ser Godoy, Erica Sosa, Richie Marrufo, Johnny Galindo, Vanessa Zuniga, Mike Peregrino, April Correa, Adri Muñiz López, Ray Ramos, Dr. Yolanda Leyva, Gris Muñoz, Jorge Gomez.

Many thanks to the EPCC Valle Verde Writing Center for being a space where I could write.

Bernard L. Conlon from EF Tours for being my guide in Ireland.

To the care providers who heard me at each appointment - Dr. Gillet, Dr. Son, Dr. Galvez, Alice Langford, and the physical therapists at UMC.

David Romo, te amo con todo mi corazón, thank you for always being there for me.

And to my family for all their love and support. Peter Tetteh Loveson, my daughter Sonnet Ashikai Loveson, my mother Tammy De La Calavera, and Rick Provencio (1951-2022) I miss you.

About the Author

Cassie Holguin-Pettinato is a Chicana poet, collage artist, and theremin musician. She is a fourth-generation resident of La Calavera, the last remaining neighborhood of El Paso's historic Smeltertown. She is the author of *The Lamb's Tail* (Bottlecap Press, 2022), a collection of poems grounded on the U.S.-Mexico borderlands that explore personal and family wounds, traumas, and disconnections. Holguin-Pettinato graduated with a bachelor's degree in Creative Writing from the University of Texas at El Paso. She co-founded Papagayo, a literary center at El Paso Community College. Holguin-Pettinato is a recipient of the Martha's Vineyard Institute of Creative Writing Poet & Author Fellowship (2024).

FLOWERSONG
P R E S S

**FlowerSong Press nurtures essential verse
from, about, and throughout the borderlands.
Literary. Lyrical. Boundless.**

Sign up for announcements about
new and upcoming titles at:

www.flowersongpress.com